The Art
of
Falling in Love:

Navigating the Ups and Downs of Relationships with Empathy, Communication, and Vulnerability

By Khaled Bouajaja

Content

Chapter 1: Meeting by Chance

It was a beautiful day in the park, the sun was shining and there was a gentle breeze blowing. The birds were singing, and the flowers were in bloom. The park was filled with people walking, jogging, and cycling. Among them was a young woman named Emily. Emily was in her mid-twenties, with long brown hair and a bright smile. She had just moved to the city and was exploring the park when she saw him.

He was tall and athletic, with broad shoulders and a chiseled jawline. He was wearing a navy blue t-shirt and black shorts, and he was jogging along the path towards her. Emily couldn't help but notice him and feel drawn to him. As he approached, she stepped to the side to let him pass, but instead, he slowed down and came to a stop beside her.

"Hi there," he said with a smile. "I couldn't help but notice you. You're new around here, right?"

Emily was surprised but delighted by his approach. "Yes, I am," she replied with a smile. "I just moved here a few weeks ago."

"That's great," he said. "I'm Ryan. Nice to meet you."

"I'm Emily," she said, extending her hand to shake his.

They stood there chatting for a few minutes, and Emily felt like they had an instant connection. They talked about where they were from, their interests, and their favorite things to do in the city. Ryan was easy to talk to, and Emily found herself feeling more and more drawn to him.

As they parted ways, Ryan asked Emily if she'd like to grab a coffee sometime. Emily agreed, and they exchanged phone numbers. As she walked away, she couldn't help but feel like she'd just had a chance encounter with destiny.

Emily and Ryan met up a few days later at a cozy coffee shop in the heart of the city. They spent hours talking, laughing, and getting to know each other better. Emily discovered that Ryan was a personal trainer at a local gym, and he was passionate about fitness and health. He also loved music and played the guitar in his spare time.

Ryan was equally smitten with Emily. He loved her easygoing nature, her sense of humor, and her passion for travel. They had so much in common, and Ryan couldn't believe he had met someone like her by chance.

After their coffee date, Emily and Ryan continued to see each other regularly. They went on hikes, explored new restaurants, and attended concerts together. Emily was amazed by how much she had in common with Ryan, and how comfortable she felt around him.

As they spent more time together, Emily and Ryan's feelings for each other deepened. They both knew they had found something special, something worth holding onto.

But their chance encounter was only the beginning of their journey. They had yet to face the challenges and obstacles that come with falling in love.

Chapter 2: A Spark of Attraction

Emily couldn't believe how lucky she was to have met Ryan. He was everything she had ever wanted in a partner - kind, funny, and smart, with a great sense of adventure. She found herself thinking about him all the time, even when they weren't together.

As their relationship grew, Emily started to notice that there was a spark of attraction between them that she couldn't ignore. She felt a pull towards Ryan that was stronger than anything she had ever felt before. Whenever he touched her or looked into her eyes, she felt a thrill run through her body.

Ryan felt the same way. He found himself wanting to be near Emily all the time, to hold her hand and kiss her. He was drawn to her energy, her intelligence, and her beauty. He knew he was falling for her, and he couldn't wait to see where their relationship would go.

One day, as they were walking through the park, Ryan took Emily's hand in his. Emily felt a jolt of electricity shoot through her body as their fingers intertwined. They stopped walking and turned to face each other.

"Emily, I have to tell you something," Ryan said, his voice low and intense. "I think I'm falling in love with you."

Emily's heart skipped a beat. She had been feeling the same way, but she didn't know how to express it. She looked up at Ryan and saw the sincerity in his eyes.

"I think I'm falling in love with you too," she said softly.

Ryan smiled and pulled her closer to him. They kissed, and it was like fireworks exploded in Emily's head. She felt a warmth spreading through her body, a feeling of happiness and contentment that she had never experienced before.

From that moment on, Emily and Ryan were inseparable. They spent every moment they could together, exploring the city and each other. They would stay up late into the night, talking about their hopes and dreams, their fears and doubts. They supported each other through everything, and their love only grew stronger.

But as much as they were drawn to each other, there were still things they didn't know about each other. They had yet to see each other's flaws, and they hadn't faced any major challenges in their relationship. That was all about to change.

One day, as they were getting ready to go out to dinner, Ryan received a phone call. Emily could tell from his face that something was wrong.

"What's going on?" she asked, her voice filled with concern.

"It's my dad," Ryan said, his voice shaky. "He's been in an accident, and he's in critical condition."

Emily put her arms around Ryan and held him close. She could feel his pain and fear, and she knew she had to be there for him.

"We'll get through this together," she said, rubbing his back soothingly.

Ryan looked up at her and saw the love in her eyes. He knew then that Emily was the one he wanted to spend the rest of his life with. She was his rock, his support, and his love.

As they left for the hospital, Emily and Ryan knew that their relationship was about to face its first major challenge. They didn't know what the future held, but they knew they had each other. And that was all that mattered.

At the hospital, Ryan was a wreck. He had never felt so scared and helpless in his life. Emily stayed by his side, holding his hand and offering words of comfort. They spent hours in the waiting room, anxiously waiting for news from the doctors.

When they finally got the news, it was both good and bad. Ryan's dad had survived the accident, but he was in a coma and his condition was critical. Ryan was devastated, but Emily remained strong for him. She knew that he needed her support now more than ever.

Over the next few weeks, Ryan spent every day at the hospital, praying for his dad's recovery. Emily would often join him, bringing him food and coffee and sitting by his side as he talked to his dad, even though he couldn't hear him.

As they spent more time together at the hospital, Emily and Ryan's love for each other grew even stronger. They had seen each other's vulnerabilities and fears, and they had supported each other through them. They knew that they could rely on each other no matter what.

Eventually, Ryan's dad woke up from his coma. He was still weak and had a long road to recovery, but he was alive. Ryan was overjoyed, and he knew that he had Emily to thank for helping him get through the ordeal.

One day, as they were walking out of the hospital, Ryan turned to Emily and took her hands in his. He looked deep into her eyes and spoke from his heart.

"Emily, you have been my rock during the toughest time of my life. I don't know what I would have done without you. I love you more than anything, and I want to spend the rest of my life with you."

Emily's heart swelled with happiness as she realized that Ryan felt the same way she did. She threw her arms around him, and they kissed passionately, the spark of attraction between them burning brighter than ever.

From that day on, Ryan and Emily's love only grew stronger. They faced many challenges over the years, but they always came out stronger on the other side. They knew that they had found true love, and they were grateful every day for the chance meeting that had brought them together.

As they stood together, watching the sun set over the city, Ryan put his arms around Emily and whispered in her ear.

"I love you more than anything in this world, Emily. You are my soulmate, and I will love you forever."

Emily smiled and leaned into him, feeling the warmth of his embrace and the strength of their love. She knew that she had found the one person who would always be there for her, no matter what life threw their way. And that was the greatest gift of all.

3. Discovering Shared Interests

After they had officially become a couple, Ryan and Emily started spending even more time together. They would go on long walks in the park, explore new neighborhoods, and try out new restaurants. They found that they had many shared interests, including hiking, photography, and cooking.

One weekend, Ryan suggested that they take a trip to a nearby national park. Emily was hesitant at first, but Ryan's enthusiasm was infectious, and she soon found herself getting excited about the trip.

They packed their bags and set off early in the morning. The drive to the park was long, but Ryan kept them entertained with stories and jokes, and before they knew it, they had arrived.

The park was breathtakingly beautiful, with towering trees, sparkling lakes, and snow-capped mountains in the distance. Ryan had planned out a few hikes for them to go on, and they spent the day exploring the trails and taking in the stunning scenery.

As they walked, Ryan pointed out interesting plants and animals, and Emily took photos of everything they saw. They stopped for a picnic lunch by a crystal-clear stream, and Emily was amazed by the delicious food Ryan had prepared.

As the day wore on, Ryan and Emily grew more and more comfortable with each other. They laughed and joked, shared stories about their childhoods, and talked about their hopes and dreams for the future.

As the sun began to set, they found themselves sitting on a rocky outcropping, watching as the sky turned shades of pink and orange. Ryan put his arm around Emily, and she leaned into him, feeling safe and happy.

"This has been the best day ever," she said softly.

Ryan turned to her and smiled. "I'm glad you enjoyed it. I love spending time with you."

They kissed as the sun disappeared behind the mountains, and Emily felt a warmth spread through her body. She knew that she was falling more deeply in love with Ryan every day.

The next day, they woke up early and went on another hike. As they walked, Emily pointed out interesting rock formations, and Ryan showed her how to identify different types of birds. They spent the day talking and laughing and taking in the natural beauty around them.

That evening, they went back to their cabin and cooked dinner together. Emily was amazed at how well Ryan could cook, and they spent the evening enjoying each other's company, sharing stories and dreams, and talking about all the adventures they wanted to have together.

As the night wore on, Ryan suggested that they go for a walk under the stars. Emily hesitated at first, but the look in Ryan's eyes was so intense that she found herself agreeing.

They walked hand in hand through the darkened forest, the only sounds the crunch of leaves beneath their feet and the occasional hoot of an owl. Emily felt a shiver run down her spine, but she knew that she was safe with Ryan by her side.

As they emerged into a clearing, Ryan stopped and turned to her. He took both of her hands in his and looked deep into her eyes.

"Emily, I have something to ask you," he said, his voice low and intense.

Emily's heart skipped a beat. She knew what was coming, and she felt a wave of happiness wash over her.

"Will you move in with me?" Ryan asked, his eyes never leaving hers.

Emily felt tears welling up in her eyes. She knew that this was a big step, but she also knew that she wanted to spend every moment with Ryan. She nodded, unable to speak.

Ryan's face broke into a wide smile, and he pulled her into a tight embrace.

"I love you so much, Emily," he whispered into her ear.

They walked back to their cabin, their steps light and happy. Emily felt like she was walking on cloud nine. She couldn't believe that she had found someone like Ryan, someone who understood her so well and made her feel so happy and loved.

Over the next few weeks, Ryan and Emily started making plans for their new life together. They looked at apartments and discussed furniture and decor. Emily was amazed at how well they worked together, how they always seemed to be on the same page.

As they settled into their new home, Ryan and Emily continued to explore their shared interests. They spent weekends hiking in the mountains, taking photos of the stunning scenery, and cooking elaborate meals together. They even signed up for a photography class together, learning new techniques and sharing tips and tricks.

As they spent more and more time together, Emily felt like she was falling deeper in love with Ryan every day. She loved the way he made her laugh, the way he always seemed to know exactly what she needed. She loved his passion for life and his adventurous spirit.

One day, as they were sitting on their balcony watching the sunset, Ryan turned to her and took her hand.

"Emily, there's something I need to tell you," he said, his voice serious.

Emily felt a twinge of anxiety. She had never heard Ryan sound so serious before.

"What is it?" she asked, her heart racing.

Ryan took a deep breath. "I've been offered a job in another city. It's a great opportunity, but it would mean moving away from here."

Emily felt her stomach drop. She couldn't imagine life without Ryan, without their shared adventures and laughter and love.

"What does that mean for us?" she asked, her voice trembling.

Ryan squeezed her hand. "I don't want to leave you, Emily. But I also don't want to pass up this opportunity. What do you think?"

Emily took a deep breath. She knew that Ryan was right, that he shouldn't pass up a great job opportunity. But the thought of being apart from him was almost unbearable.

"I want you to take the job," she said finally, her voice low. "I'll miss you like crazy, but I know that this is important for you."

Ryan pulled her into a tight embrace. "I love you so much, Emily," he whispered.

Over the next few weeks, Ryan prepared for his move, packing up his belongings and saying goodbye to friends and family. Emily tried to be strong, but every time she thought about him leaving, she felt a lump form in her throat.

On the day of his departure, Emily drove Ryan to the airport. They held each other tightly, both trying to hold back tears.

"I'll call you every day," Ryan promised. "We'll make this work, I know we will."

Emily nodded, unable to speak. She watched as Ryan disappeared through the security gate, her heart breaking.

For the first few days, Emily tried to keep busy. She threw herself into her work and spent time with friends, trying to distract herself from the emptiness she felt inside. But no matter what she did, she couldn't shake the feeling that something was missing.

Every night, Ryan called her, telling her about his new job and the new city he was living in. Emily listened, trying to be happy for him, but all she could think about was how much she missed him.

One night, as they were talking on the phone, Ryan suggested that Emily come visit him. Emily's heart leapt at the thought of seeing him again, of being able to hold him and kiss him and tell him how much she loved him.

"I'd love to," she said eagerly.

Ryan made all the arrangements, and a few weeks later, Emily found herself standing in the airport terminal, waiting for Ryan to arrive.

As she watched him come through the gate, Emily's heart raced. She ran towards him, throwing her arms around his neck and kissing him deeply. It was like no time had passed at all, and they were right back where they left off.

Over the next few days, Emily and Ryan explored the city together. They went to museums, tried new restaurants, and visited all the tourist spots. It was like they were on a second honeymoon.

As they lay in bed one night, Ryan turned to Emily and took her hand.

"Emily, I know that being apart from each other is hard," he said softly. "But I also know that I want to spend the rest of my life with you. Will you marry me?"

Emily felt her heart skip a beat. She had always dreamed of being proposed to in a romantic setting, with flowers and candles and all the works. But here they were, in a simple hotel room, and it was perfect.

"Yes, Ryan. Yes, I'll marry you," she said, tears streaming down her face.

Ryan pulled out a small box from his pocket and opened it to reveal a simple but beautiful diamond ring. Emily couldn't believe how perfect it was.

Over the next few days, Emily and Ryan basked in the glow of their engagement. They talked about their future together, about where they wanted to live and what kind of family they wanted to have. It was like everything had fallen into place.

When it was time for Emily to go back home, she felt a sense of sadness wash over her. She didn't want to leave Ryan behind, but she knew that they had to be apart for a little while longer.

As they hugged goodbye, Ryan whispered in her ear, "I'll see you soon, my love."

Emily smiled, feeling a sense of hope for their future together. She knew that they could make this work, that they were meant to be together.

Over the next few months, Emily and Ryan continued to talk every day. They made plans for their wedding and discussed their future together. Emily was thrilled to be planning her future with the love of her life.

Finally, the day came for Ryan to come back home. Emily waited anxiously at the airport, feeling like a teenager waiting for her first date. When Ryan walked through the gate, Emily ran to him, throwing her arms around his neck and kissing him deeply.

From that moment on, they were inseparable. They continued to explore their shared interests and tried new things together. They knew that they had found something special, something that was worth fighting for.

As they stood at the altar on their wedding day, Emily looked into Ryan's eyes and knew that she had found her soulmate. They exchanged their vows, promising to love and cherish each other for the rest of their lives.

As they danced their first dance as husband and wife, Emily knew that they had discovered their shared interests, but more importantly, they had discovered a love that would last a lifetime.

4. Learning to Communicate

Emily and Ryan had been married for almost a year, and they were still in the honeymoon phase. They had settled into married life easily, and they were happier than ever. However, there was one thing that Emily had noticed - they were terrible at communicating.

It wasn't that they didn't talk to each other; they talked all the time. But they often talked past each other, not really listening to what the other was saying. It was like they were in their own little worlds, and they weren't really connecting.

Emily knew that communication was essential in any relationship, especially a marriage. So, she decided to take action.

One day, she sat Ryan down and said, "We need to talk about something important. I think we need to work on our communication skills."

Ryan looked at her, a little confused. "What do you mean?" he asked.

"I mean that we need to learn how to really listen to each other and understand what the other person is saying. We often talk past each other, and I think that's causing some problems."

Ryan nodded slowly. "I see what you mean," he said. "What do you suggest we do?"

Emily had been thinking about this for a while, and she had a few ideas. "Well, I think we should start by really listening to each other when we talk. That means putting away our phones and really focusing on the other person. We should also repeat back what the other person said to make sure we understand correctly."

Ryan looked a little skeptical. "Won't that be a little awkward?" he asked.

Emily shrugged. "Maybe at first, but I think it's important. We need to make sure we're on the same page about things, especially when it comes to big decisions."

Ryan nodded slowly. "Okay, I'm willing to try."

Over the next few weeks, Emily and Ryan made a conscious effort to improve their communication skills. They put away their phones when they were talking, and they really focused on what the other person was saying. They also repeated back what the other person said to make sure they understood correctly.

At first, it was a little awkward. They stumbled over their words and had to ask each other to repeat things several times. But slowly, they started to get the hang of it. They began to understand each other better and to really connect on a deeper level.

It wasn't just the big things they talked about, either. They talked about their day at work, their hopes and dreams, and even the small things that annoyed them. They realized that it was the little things that could build up and cause resentment, so they made sure to address them as they came up.

One day, Ryan came home from work looking a little upset. Emily noticed right away and asked him what was wrong. At first, Ryan shrugged it off, saying it was nothing. But Emily persisted, and eventually, Ryan opened up about a problem he was having at work.

As Ryan talked, Emily listened carefully, asking questions and repeating back what he said to make sure she understood. When Ryan was finished, Emily gave him a hug and told him how proud she was of him for handling the situation so well.

Ryan looked surprised. "You're not mad?" he asked.

"Why would I be mad?" Emily asked, confused.

Ryan shrugged. "I don't know. I just thought you might be upset about something that happened at work."

Emily shook her head. "No, I'm not upset. I'm just glad you told me about it. That's what marriage is all about, right? Supporting each other through the ups and downs."

Ryan smiled, feeling a sense of relief. "You're right," he said. "I'm so glad we're learning to communicate better."

As time went on, Emily and Ryan's communication skills continued to improve. They were able to have difficult conversations without getting defensive or shutting down. They also started to understand each other's communication styles better, which helped them to avoid misunderstandings.

Emily was surprised to discover that she often communicated her feelings through actions rather than words. For example, if she was feeling upset, she would withdraw and become quiet. Ryan, on the other hand, tended to become defensive when he felt criticized.

Once they understood these patterns, they were able to work on them. Emily made an effort to express her feelings verbally, and Ryan worked on not becoming defensive when Emily brought up something that was bothering her.

It wasn't always easy, of course. There were times when they fell back into their old patterns of communication. But they always made an effort to get back on track.

One day, Emily and Ryan were sitting on the couch, enjoying a quiet evening at home. Ryan was scrolling through his phone, and Emily was reading a book. Suddenly, Ryan put his phone down and turned to Emily.

"I've been thinking," he said. "I know we've been working on our communication skills, but I feel like there's still something missing."

Emily looked up, surprised. "What do you mean?"

"I mean that we're good at talking to each other, but we don't really talk about the big things. Like our goals for the future, or our hopes and dreams."

Emily nodded slowly. "I see what you mean. We've been so focused on improving our day-to-day communication that we haven't really talked about the bigger picture."

Ryan smiled. "Exactly. So, I was thinking that we should have a date night where we just talk about all of that stuff. No phones, no distractions, just us."

Emily smiled back. "I love that idea. Let's do it."

And so, the next Saturday, Emily and Ryan had a date night. They went out to dinner and then took a walk in the park. As they walked, they talked about their hopes and dreams for the future. They talked about where they wanted to live, what kind of careers they wanted to have, and whether or not they wanted children.

It was a deep and meaningful conversation, and it brought them even closer together. They realized that they had a lot of shared goals and values, and that they were both committed to making their marriage work.

As they walked back to their car, Emily took Ryan's hand. "Thank you for tonight," she said. "I feel like we really connected on a deeper level."

Ryan smiled. "Me too. I love you."

"I love you too," Emily said.

And with that, they drove home, feeling more connected than ever. They knew that they still had work to do when it came to communication, but they were confident that they could handle whatever came their way as long as they were working on it together.

5. The First Date

Emily and Ryan had been married for over a year, but they still enjoyed going on dates. They both believed that it was important to make time for each other and to keep their relationship fresh and exciting.

One Saturday afternoon, Ryan surprised Emily by telling her that he had planned a special date night for them. He didn't give her any details, but he told her to dress up and be ready by 7 pm.

Emily was intrigued and excited. She spent the afternoon getting ready, trying on different outfits and experimenting with her makeup. She finally settled on a black dress that Ryan had given her for their first anniversary, paired with a pair of high heels.

When Ryan arrived to pick her up, Emily's heart skipped a beat. He looked so handsome in his suit and tie, and he had a bouquet of flowers for her.

"Wow," Emily said, taking the flowers from Ryan. "You look amazing."

"You look stunning," Ryan said, kissing her on the cheek. "Are you ready for our surprise date?"

Emily nodded eagerly. "Yes, I'm so excited."

Ryan drove them to a fancy restaurant in the heart of the city. Emily had never been there before, but she had heard of it. It was known for its exquisite cuisine and romantic atmosphere.

As they were seated at their table, Emily couldn't help but feel giddy with excitement. She loved spending time with Ryan, and she was looking forward to a night of good food, good wine, and good conversation.

They ordered their drinks and perused the menu, making small talk about their day. But as the night wore on, the conversation turned more serious.

"Emily," Ryan said, taking her hand across the table. "I have something to tell you."

Emily's heart skipped a beat. She had a feeling she knew what was coming, and she was both excited and nervous.

"I love you," Ryan said, looking into her eyes. "More than anything in this world. And I want to spend the rest of my life with you."

Emily's eyes filled with tears. "Ryan," she said, her voice choked with emotion. "I love you too."

Ryan reached into his pocket and pulled out a small velvet box. He opened it to reveal a beautiful diamond ring.

"Emily," he said, his voice shaking with emotion. "Will you marry me again? Will you renew our vows and promise to spend the rest of your life with me?"

Emily was speechless. She looked at the ring, then back at Ryan's eyes. She knew that this was a moment that she would remember for the rest of her life.

"Yes," she finally said, her voice barely above a whisper. "Yes, I will."

Ryan slipped the ring onto Emily's finger, and they both leaned across the table to kiss each other. The other patrons in the restaurant applauded, and the waitstaff brought them a bottle of champagne to celebrate.

As they toasted to their love and commitment, Emily felt more in love with Ryan than ever before. She knew that their marriage wasn't always going to be easy, but she also knew that they were in it together for the long haul.

As they left the restaurant, Emily took Ryan's hand. "Thank you for tonight," she said. "It was perfect."

Ryan smiled. "I'm just happy that I get to spend the rest of my life with you."

And with that, they walked hand in hand into the night, ready to face whatever challenges and adventures lay ahead of them.

The following weeks were a flurry of activity as Emily and Ryan planned their vow renewal ceremony. They decided to keep it small, with just their closest family and friends in attendance. They chose a beautiful venue in the countryside, surrounded by lush greenery and blooming flowers.

Emily found herself getting emotional as she wrote her vows, reflecting on the years they had spent together and the love they had shared. She wanted to make sure that Ryan knew just how much he meant to her and how grateful she was to have him in her life.

On the day of the ceremony, Emily felt a mix of nerves and excitement as she put on her white dress and veil. She felt like a bride all over again, and her heart swelled with love as she walked down the aisle towards Ryan.

He looked dashing in his suit, and his eyes shone with emotion as he watched Emily approach him. They held hands as they exchanged their vows, tears streaming down their faces.

"I promise to love you more each day, to support you through thick and thin, and to always be your partner in life," Ryan said, his voice full of emotion.

"And I promise to be your best friend, your confidante, and your forever partner," Emily replied, her heart overflowing with love.

As they exchanged rings and kissed, their family and friends cheered, and they walked back down the aisle together as husband and wife once again.

The reception was filled with laughter, tears, and heartfelt speeches from their loved ones. Emily and Ryan danced together under the stars, feeling more in love than ever before.

As the night came to a close, Emily felt like she was on cloud nine. She knew that renewing their vows wasn't going to change their relationship overnight, but it was a symbol of their commitment to each other and a reminder of the love they shared.

In the weeks and months that followed, Emily and Ryan continued to work on their marriage. They made time for each other, communicated openly and honestly, and found new ways to keep their relationship fresh and exciting.

They went on romantic getaways, tried new hobbies together, and supported each other through the ups and downs of life. They knew that marriage wasn't always going to be easy, but they were in it for the long haul.

And through it all, they never forgot the spark of attraction that had brought them together in the first place. They knew that they were lucky to have found each other by chance, and they were grateful for the love that had grown between them over the years.`a

Emily and Ryan's renewed commitment to each other brought a new level of closeness and intimacy to their relationship. They talked openly about their feelings, fears, and hopes for the future. They took the time to listen to each other and support each other's dreams.

As they continued to discover shared interests, they found new ways to connect with each other. They took dance lessons together, went hiking in the mountains, and even tried skydiving. Emily never thought she would be brave enough to jump out of a plane, but with Ryan by her side, she felt like she could conquer anything.

Their communication skills improved, and they learned to resolve conflicts in a healthy and respectful way. They no longer let small disagreements turn into big arguments. Instead, they took a step back, listened to each other's perspectives, and found a way to compromise.

Their renewed commitment to each other also brought a new level of passion to their physical relationship. They made time to be intimate with each other, and they explored new ways to bring pleasure and excitement to their bedroom.

But it wasn't all sunshine and roses. There were times when Emily and Ryan faced challenges that tested their commitment to each other. They lost loved ones, faced health scares, and struggled with work-related stress. But they always leaned on each other for support and found a way to get through the tough times together.

As the years passed, Emily and Ryan's love for each other only grew stronger. They celebrated their milestones together, including their 10th, 20th, and 30th anniversaries. They renewed their vows again on their 25th anniversary, surrounded by their children and grandchildren.

Looking back on their journey together, Emily realized that meeting Ryan by chance was one of the best things that had ever happened to her. She felt grateful for every moment they had shared together, and she knew that their love would only continue to grow in the years to come.

Ryan felt the same way. He knew that he had found his soulmate in Emily, and he was grateful for the chance encounter that had brought them together. He knew that their love was special, and he was committed to cherishing and nurturing it for the rest of his life.

As they sat together on their front porch, holding hands and watching the sunset, Emily and Ryan knew that their love story was far from over. They had grown together, laughed together, and cried together. They had faced the highs and lows of life side by side, and they knew that they would continue to do so for as long as they lived.

And as they looked out at the world together, Emily and Ryan knew that there was nothing they couldn't conquer as long as they had each other.

6. Overcoming Obstacles

Emily and Ryan had been married for 15 years when they faced one of the biggest challenges of their relationship. Ryan had been offered a job opportunity in another state, and they would have to move away from their hometown and everything they had known for their entire lives.

Emily was hesitant about the move, but she knew how important this opportunity was for Ryan's career. She also knew that they could handle any challenge as long as they were together.

Together, they made the decision to take the job and move to a new city. The move was difficult, but they worked together to make the transition as smooth as possible. They found a new home, made new friends, and started to build a new life in their new city.

But the move had taken a toll on their relationship. Emily was struggling to adjust to their new surroundings and felt isolated and alone. Ryan was working long hours at his new job and didn't have as much time to spend with Emily as he used to.

Their communication started to break down, and they found themselves arguing more often than not. Emily felt like Ryan wasn't giving her the attention she needed, and Ryan felt like Emily was being too clingy and needy.

One night, they had a big fight that brought all their underlying issues to the surface. They both felt hurt and frustrated, but instead of letting the argument escalate, they decided to take a step back and take some time to cool off.

The next day, they sat down and had a heart-to-heart conversation. They both acknowledged their shortcomings and promised to work on their communication and relationship.

They started to make time for each other again. They went on dates, took walks in their new neighborhood, and explored their new city together. They also made an effort to listen to each other and support each other's needs.

As they worked through their issues, they realized that the move had been a blessing in disguise. It had forced them to confront their problems and work on their relationship in a way that they might not have done otherwise.

Over time, they adjusted to their new life and found that they had grown closer than ever before. They were proud of the way they had worked through their challenges and strengthened their relationship.

Looking back on that time in their lives, Emily and Ryan knew that they could overcome anything as long as they were together. They had faced one of the biggest challenges of their relationship and come out the other side stronger and more committed than ever before.

And as they looked out at their new city together, Emily and Ryan knew that they had made the right decision. They had taken a chance on each other, and it had paid off in ways they could have never imagined.

As they stood by the car, Emily could see the look of dismay on Ryan's face. She could tell that he was worried about the loss of his laptop and the impact it would have on his work.

"We'll figure it out," Emily reassured him, putting a hand on his shoulder. "We'll find a way to get your work files back."

Ryan nodded, but Emily could still see the worry in his eyes. They drove back to their apartment in silence, both lost in thought.

Once they got home, Emily made a cup of tea and sat down with Ryan at the kitchen table. "Let's try to figure out what we can do," she said gently. "Maybe we can contact the laptop company and see if they can retrieve your files?"

Ryan sighed. "I don't know if that will work," he said. "I should have backed up my files."

Emily didn't want to make things worse by pointing out the mistake. Instead, she brainstormed with Ryan on other potential solutions. They thought of a few options, such as hiring a data recovery service, but they were all expensive and might not guarantee the retrieval of all of Ryan's work.

As they talked, Emily realized that she had a skill that could be useful in this situation. She had taken a computer science course in college and had learned some basics of data recovery. She didn't know if she could solve the problem, but she was willing to try.

"I might be able to help," she said hesitantly. "I learned some data recovery basics in college."

Ryan looked at her skeptically. "Are you sure you can do it?" he asked.

Emily hesitated, but then she remembered how Ryan had stepped out of his comfort zone for her at the music festival. She wanted to do the same for him.

"I'll try my best," she said with determination. "I can't guarantee anything, but it's worth a shot."

Ryan looked grateful, but still worried. "Thank you," he said softly.

Emily spent the rest of the evening working on the laptop, trying different recovery methods she had learned in college. It was frustrating and tedious work, but she was determined to help Ryan retrieve his files.

Finally, after several hours of work, Emily managed to recover most of Ryan's work files. They were not all perfect, but it was better than losing everything. Ryan was ecstatic and grateful, and Emily felt a sense of accomplishment and satisfaction.

As they sat on the couch together, Ryan put his arm around Emily and pulled her close. "Thank you," he whispered, "you saved my work."

Emily smiled and leaned her head on his shoulder. "I would do anything for you," she said softly.

This experience brought them even closer together, as they learned to rely on each other and work together to overcome obstacles. They realized that they made a great team, and that they could count on each other no matter what.

After the laptop incident, Ryan and Emily's relationship continued to grow stronger. They were more comfortable around each other and began to share more about their past and their hopes for the future.

They discovered that they both loved to travel and explore new places. Ryan had always wanted to visit Japan, while Emily had dreamt of backpacking through Europe. They made a plan to save up money and make these trips a reality someday.

They also found that they shared a love for the outdoors. Ryan had grown up camping and hiking with his family, while Emily had discovered a passion for nature during a college camping trip. They started going on weekend hikes together and exploring nearby state parks.

But most importantly, they learned how to communicate with each other more effectively. They learned to listen to each other's opinions and feelings without judgment, and to express themselves honestly and openly.

One evening, as they were cooking dinner together, Emily broached a sensitive topic.

"Ryan, I've been thinking about something," she said hesitantly. "I want to talk to you about it."

Ryan looked up from chopping vegetables. "Sure, what is it?"

"It's about our future," Emily said, taking a deep breath. "I know we haven't been together for very long, but I want to know what you think about us moving in together."

Ryan paused for a moment, considering her proposal. "I've actually been thinking about that too," he admitted. "I think it could be a good idea."

Emily smiled, feeling relieved. "Really?"

"Yeah," Ryan said, grinning. "I love spending time with you, and I think it would be great to wake up next to you every morning."

They spent the rest of the evening discussing logistics and making plans for moving in together. It was a big step for their relationship, but they were excited and ready for it.

A few weeks later, they found a cute apartment in a trendy neighborhood and moved in together. It was an adjustment at first, as they learned to share a space and adapt to each other's routines. But they were happy and in love, and they knew they had made the right decision.

Their shared interests and communication skills continued to strengthen their bond. They learned how to compromise and support each other through challenges and difficult times.

One day, while they were on a hike, Ryan stopped and turned to Emily. "I have something to ask you," he said, getting down on one knee.

Emily gasped, her heart pounding. "What is it?" she asked, her eyes wide with anticipation.

"Emily, I love you more than anything in this world," Ryan said, taking her hand. "Will you marry me?"

Tears filled Emily's eyes as she nodded eagerly. "Yes, yes, of course I will!" she exclaimed, throwing her arms around Ryan's neck.

They hugged and kissed, surrounded by the beauty of nature. It was a perfect moment, and they knew that they had found true love in each other.

7. Building Trust

Ryan and Emily had been married for almost a year, and their love continued to thrive. They had built a strong foundation of communication, shared interests, and mutual respect, but they knew that trust was also a vital component of any successful relationship.

Trust was something that was important to both Ryan and Emily, but they had different experiences with it in the past. Ryan had been hurt by an ex-partner who had cheated on him, while Emily had struggled with trust issues due to a difficult childhood.

They knew that building trust would take time and effort, but they were committed to doing so. They started by being honest with each other about their feelings and concerns. If one of them felt uneasy or worried about something, they would talk it out and find a solution together.

They also made an effort to keep their promises and commitments. If Ryan said he would be home by a certain time, he made sure to stick to that. If Emily promised to do something, she followed through.

They also made an effort to give each other the benefit of the doubt. If one of them did something that could be misinterpreted or taken the wrong way, they would assume that it was not intentional and discuss it calmly and rationally.

One day, while Ryan was at work, Emily received a phone call from an unknown number. The caller claimed to be a woman that Ryan had been seeing on the side and asked Emily how it felt to be married to a cheater.

Emily's heart raced as she hung up the phone. She felt a wave of panic and insecurity wash over her. She trusted Ryan, but the call had planted a seed of doubt in her mind.

She called Ryan immediately, feeling a knot form in her stomach. "Ryan, I just received a call from someone claiming to be your mistress," she said, trying to keep her voice steady.

Ryan was shocked and appalled. "What? That's ridiculous! Emily, I would never cheat on you," he exclaimed.

Emily could hear the sincerity in his voice and felt a sense of relief wash over her. They talked for a while longer, with Ryan reassuring her that he loved her and that the call was just a cruel prank.

After they hung up, Emily realized that their trust in each other had grown stronger. Ryan had been honest and transparent with her, and she had chosen to believe him.

Over time, they continued to build on this foundation of trust. They learned to be vulnerable with each other and share their fears and insecurities. They worked through challenges and difficult situations together, always coming out stronger on the other side.

As they celebrated their second wedding anniversary, Ryan surprised Emily with a weekend getaway to a romantic bed and breakfast. As they sat by the fire, sipping wine and reminiscing about their journey together, Ryan looked into Emily's eyes and said, "I trust you with my whole heart, Emily. You are my best friend, my partner, and my soulmate."

Emily smiled, feeling a sense of gratitude and love wash over her. "I trust you too, Ryan. You are my rock, my support system, and my forever." They held hands and gazed into the fire, knowing that their love and trust would continue to grow stronger with each passing day.

As they returned home from their weekend getaway, Ryan and Emily knew that building trust was an ongoing process. They made a commitment to continue to be open and honest with each other and to communicate regularly.

They also recognized that trust was not just about fidelity but also about respecting each other's boundaries and being there for each other during difficult times. They supported each other's goals and aspirations, and they knew that they could always count on each other.

One day, Emily received a job offer in another state. The offer was a great opportunity, but it would mean that they would have to move away from their family and friends. Ryan knew how important this opportunity was for Emily, but he was also worried about leaving their support system behind.

They talked it out and came up with a plan that worked for both of them. They decided to make the move but to also make an effort to stay connected with their loved ones. They made regular trips back home and kept in touch through phone calls and video chats.

As they settled into their new home, Ryan and Emily continued to build on their trust. They met new people and made new friends, but they always put each other first. They made an effort to continue to grow and learn together, never taking each other for granted.

Years went by, and they celebrated their tenth wedding anniversary with a trip to Europe. As they strolled through the streets of Paris, Ryan turned to Emily and said, "I never imagined that our chance encounter at that coffee shop would lead to this. You are my partner, my best friend, and the love of my life."

Emily smiled, feeling grateful for the journey they had been on together. "I feel the same way, Ryan. Our love and trust have only grown stronger over the years, and I am excited to see what the future holds for us."

As they embraced each other, Ryan and Emily knew that building trust was an ongoing process, but they were committed to doing so. They had learned that trust was about honesty, respect, and communication, and they had built a strong foundation of trust that would last a lifetime.

In the years that followed, Ryan and Emily continued to face challenges and obstacles, but they always faced them together. They had learned that building trust was not a one-time thing, but rather a continuous effort.

They also realized that building trust was not just about what they did for each other, but also about the way they treated themselves. They took care of their physical and mental health, pursued their interests, and set goals for themselves. This allowed them to be their best selves and to show up fully in their relationship.

As they entered their golden years, Ryan and Emily looked back on their life together with pride and contentment. They had built a strong and loving relationship that had stood the test of time. They had faced challenges and overcome obstacles, but they had always done so together.

And while they knew that their journey was far from over, they were grateful for the love and trust that they had built and were excited to continue growing and learning together.

In conclusion, building trust is a crucial aspect of any successful relationship. Trust is built through honesty, communication, and mutual respect. It is not a one-time thing but rather a continuous effort that requires both partners to be committed to each other's growth and well-being. By investing in building trust, couples can create a strong and loving foundation for a lifetime of happiness together.

8. Intimacy and Vulnerability

Ryan and Emily had always been close, but as they approached their thirtieth wedding anniversary, they realized that they had yet to fully explore the depths of intimacy and vulnerability in their relationship.

For years, they had kept certain thoughts and feelings to themselves, afraid to open up and be vulnerable with each other. They had also let the stress and responsibilities of daily life get in the way of physical intimacy.

But they knew that if they wanted to continue to grow together, they needed to be willing to be vulnerable with each other and to prioritize their physical connection.

They started by setting aside time each week to connect on a deeper level. They made an effort to truly listen to each other without judgment and to share their fears, hopes, and dreams.

As they opened up to each other, they began to feel more connected than ever before. They laughed and cried together, and they discovered new things about each other that they had never known.

They also made an effort to prioritize physical intimacy, even when they were busy or stressed. They made time for romantic dates and weekend getaways, and they experimented with new ways to connect physically.

As they explored intimacy and vulnerability in their relationship, Ryan and Emily discovered that they were able to connect on a much deeper level than they ever had before. They felt more secure in their love for each other and more confident in their ability to weather any storm that came their way.

They also realized that vulnerability and intimacy required trust and communication. They had to be willing to trust each other with their deepest thoughts and feelings, and they had to communicate openly and honestly with each other.

Over time, their commitment to intimacy and vulnerability became a natural part of their relationship. They continued to explore new ways to connect physically and emotionally, and they continued to prioritize their relationship above all else.

As they approached their fortieth wedding anniversary, Ryan and Emily knew that they had built a strong and loving foundation for a lifetime of happiness together. They had learned that intimacy and vulnerability were not weaknesses, but rather strengths that allowed them to connect on a deeper level and to build a relationship that would stand the test of time.

In conclusion, intimacy and vulnerability are essential aspects of any successful relationship. They require trust, communication, and a willingness to be open and honest with each other. By prioritizing intimacy and vulnerability, couples can deepen their connection and build a strong and loving foundation for a lifetime of happiness together.

However, building intimacy and vulnerability in a relationship is not always easy. It can be challenging to let down your guard and share your deepest thoughts and feelings with someone else. It can also be difficult to prioritize physical intimacy in the midst of busy schedules and daily stresses.

Ryan and Emily knew this firsthand. It took time and effort to build intimacy and vulnerability in their relationship. They had to be patient with each other and willing to work through any obstacles that came their way.

They also had to be willing to address any issues that arose in their relationship. They couldn't simply sweep problems under the rug and hope they would go away. Instead, they had to be willing to have difficult conversations and to work together to find solutions.

This required a high degree of trust and communication. They had to be willing to trust each other with their deepest thoughts and feelings, and they had to be willing to communicate openly and honestly with each other.

Over time, as they continued to work on building intimacy and vulnerability, they found that it became easier and more natural. They began to feel more comfortable sharing their thoughts and feelings with each other, and they found that physical intimacy became a source of comfort and joy in their relationship.

They also discovered that building intimacy and vulnerability in their relationship had a positive impact on other areas of their lives. They felt more connected to each other and more confident in their ability to handle any challenges that came their way.

In addition, they found that their commitment to intimacy and vulnerability inspired them to be more vulnerable and authentic in other areas of their lives. They became more willing to take risks and to be true to themselves, knowing that they had a strong and supportive partner by their side.

In conclusion, building intimacy and vulnerability in a relationship is a process that requires time, effort, and a willingness to be open and honest with each other. It can be challenging, but it is also incredibly rewarding. By prioritizing intimacy and vulnerability, couples can deepen their connection and build a strong and loving foundation for a lifetime of happiness together.

9. Deepening Connection

As Ryan and Emily continued to build intimacy and vulnerability in their relationship, they found that their connection deepened in unexpected ways. They began to understand each other on a deeper level, and they felt a sense of closeness and comfort that they had never experienced before.

One way that they deepened their connection was by spending quality time together. They made it a priority to have regular date nights, where they could focus on each other and enjoy each other's company without distractions.

They also found that shared experiences helped to deepen their connection. They enjoyed trying new activities together, such as hiking, cooking, or taking dance lessons. These experiences gave them the opportunity to learn more about each other's interests and to create lasting memories together.

Another way that they deepened their connection was by being supportive of each other's goals and dreams. They encouraged each other to pursue their passions, and they were there to celebrate each other's successes and to offer comfort and support during times of disappointment.

In addition, they found that practicing gratitude and appreciation helped to deepen their connection. They made a habit of expressing gratitude for each other's positive qualities and actions, and they took time to appreciate the little things that made their relationship special.

As their connection deepened, Ryan and Emily found that they felt more comfortable being themselves around each other. They could share their thoughts and feelings without fear of judgment or rejection, and they felt accepted and loved for who they were.

This deepened connection also helped them to navigate any challenges that arose in their relationship. They knew that they could count on each other for support and understanding, and they were willing to work together to find solutions to any problems that came their way.

In conclusion, deepening connection in a relationship requires a willingness to invest time and effort into the relationship. By spending quality time together, sharing experiences, supporting each other's goals and dreams, and practicing gratitude and appreciation, couples can deepen their connection and create a strong and loving foundation for their relationship.

Ryan and Emily were sitting on the couch, snuggled up together, enjoying a lazy Sunday afternoon.

"I feel like we've gotten so much closer lately," Emily said, looking up at Ryan.

"I know what you mean," Ryan replied, wrapping his arm around her. "I feel like we understand each other better than ever before."

"I think it's because we've been spending so much quality time together," Emily said. "We've really made an effort to prioritize our relationship."

"Yeah, and we've been trying new things together, which has been really fun," Ryan added.

"I also appreciate how supportive you are of my goals and dreams," Emily said. "It means a lot to me that you're always there to cheer me on."

"Of course, I want you to be happy and fulfilled," Ryan said, kissing her forehead.

Emily smiled and snuggled in closer to Ryan. "I feel so comfortable being myself around you," she said. "I don't have to pretend or put on a front. I can just be me."

"I feel the same way," Ryan said. "And I know that we can work through anything that comes our way because we have such a strong connection."

Emily nodded. "I'm grateful for you every day," she said.

"I'm grateful for you too," Ryan said, pulling her in for a kiss. "I love you."

"I love you too," Emily said, beaming.

As they continued to snuggle on the couch, Ryan and Emily began to talk about their future together. They had both been hesitant to broach the subject before, but now that their connection was so strong, they felt ready to have an open and honest conversation.

"I know we haven't talked about this before, but I've been thinking a lot about our future together," Ryan said, nervously.

Emily turned to him, sensing the seriousness in his voice. "What about our future?" she asked.

"Well, I love you and I can't imagine my life without you," Ryan said. "And I was wondering if you've ever thought about, you know, getting married someday?"

Emily's eyes widened in surprise, but then a smile spread across her face. "I have thought about it," she said. "And I love you too. I can't imagine my life without you either."

Ryan felt a wave of relief wash over him. "So, does that mean you'd want to get married someday?" he asked, hesitantly.

Emily took a deep breath. "Yes, I do," she said, looking into his eyes. "But I don't want to rush into anything. I want to make sure we're both ready and that we're doing it for the right reasons."

Ryan nodded in agreement. "Absolutely, I don't want to rush anything either," he said. "I just wanted to make sure we were on the same page."

Emily smiled and leaned in to give him a kiss. "I'm so glad we can talk about these things," she said.

"Me too," Ryan said, feeling a weight lifted off his shoulders. "I just want to make sure we're always honest and open with each other."

"Agreed," Emily said, snuggling back into his embrace. "I love you, Ryan."

"I love you too, Emily," Ryan said, holding her tight. They both knew that their deepening connection had brought them to this moment, and they were excited to see where their future would take them.

10. Celebrating Milestones

As Ryan and Emily's relationship continued to flourish, they began to reach important milestones together. They celebrated their first anniversary with a romantic weekend getaway, exchanging heartfelt gifts and reminiscing about all the special moments they had shared over the past year.

As time went on, they continued to support each other through both happy and difficult times. Ryan was there for Emily when she landed her dream job, and she was there for him when he lost his beloved grandfather.

They celebrated each other's birthdays, holidays, and other special occasions with thoughtful gestures and loving words. Ryan surprised Emily with a homemade dinner and a romantic evening at home on her birthday, while Emily planned a surprise weekend trip to Ryan's favorite camping spot for his.

They also made a point to celebrate their personal achievements together. When Ryan ran his first marathon, Emily was waiting for him at the finish line with a congratulatory banner and a big hug. And when Emily finished writing her first novel, Ryan toasted her with champagne and a heartfelt speech at a celebratory dinner.

Through it all, their love for each other only continued to grow. They felt grateful for every moment they shared and for the milestones they had reached together.

"I can't believe how far we've come," Emily said one night, as they lay in bed together. "It feels like just yesterday we met by chance."

Ryan turned to her, his eyes filled with love. "I know, but look at everything we've accomplished together," he said. "I can't wait to see what the future holds for us."

"Me too," Emily said, snuggling closer to him. "As long as we have each other, I know we can handle anything that comes our way."

And with that, they fell asleep in each other's arms, looking forward to the next milestone they would reach together.

As the months went on, Ryan and Emily continued to support each other through new challenges and obstacles. They made sure to communicate openly and honestly about their feelings and concerns, and always made time for each other despite their busy schedules.

One day, as they were sitting together on the couch, Emily brought up a topic that had been on her mind for a while.

"Ryan, I feel like we've been together for a long time now, and I love you more than anything," she said, looking at him earnestly. "But I'm starting to wonder if we're on the same page about our future together."

Ryan furrowed his brow in confusion. "What do you mean?" he asked.

"I mean, have you thought about where you see us in the next few years?" Emily asked. "Do you see us getting married someday, or starting a family?"

Ryan hesitated for a moment, taking in her words. "Honestly, I haven't really thought about it," he admitted. "But I do know that I love you more than anything, and I can't imagine my life without you."

Emily smiled, feeling a sense of relief. "I feel the same way, Ryan. And I know that we have a lot of time to figure things out. But it's important to me that we're on the same page about what we want for our future together."

Ryan nodded, understanding. "I agree, and I promise to think more about what I want for us. But right now, I know that I want to continue to love and support you in every way that I can."

Emily smiled, feeling reassured by Ryan's words. "And I want to do the same for you," she said, leaning in to kiss him.

Their conversation marked a turning point in their relationship, as they both realized the importance of being open and honest about their desires for the future. They continued to deepen their connection and build trust in each other, knowing that their love would only continue to grow stronger with each passing day.

As they fell asleep that night, wrapped in each other's arms, they both felt a sense of peace and contentment knowing that they were on this journey together. And they looked forward to celebrating many more milestones in the future, whatever they may be.

Ryan and Emily had been dating for over two years when they celebrated their first anniversary. They decided to take a trip together to a cabin in the mountains, where they spent a weekend hiking, cooking, and relaxing by the fireplace.

As they sat outside under the stars, Ryan brought out a bottle of wine and two glasses. "Here's to us, and to all the adventures we've had together so far," he said, raising his glass to Emily.

Emily smiled, feeling grateful for the love and support that Ryan had given her over the past year. "And here's to many more adventures to come," she said, clinking her glass against his.

As the night went on, they talked about their favorite memories from the past year, and made plans for the future. They talked about traveling to new places, trying new things, and building a life together.

Over the next few years, Ryan and Emily celebrated many more milestones together. They marked their second and third anniversaries with special trips and romantic gestures, and cheered each other on through new job opportunities, personal achievements, and life changes.

They also faced their fair share of challenges and obstacles, but they always came out stronger on the other side. Whether it was a difficult conversation or a tough decision, they tackled it together with love and respect.

And as they approached their fourth anniversary, Ryan knew that he wanted to take things to the next level. He spent weeks planning the perfect proposal, choosing the perfect location and ring to make the moment unforgettable.

On a warm summer evening, Ryan took Emily to a beautiful overlook where they had watched the sunset many times before. As the sun dipped below the horizon, Ryan got down on one knee and asked Emily to spend the rest of her life with him.

Emily's eyes filled with tears as she said yes, feeling overwhelmed with love and happiness. They held each other close, knowing that they had found their soulmate in each other.

And as they looked forward to their future together, Ryan and Emily knew that they would continue to celebrate all of life's milestones, big and small, knowing that their love would only continue to grow stronger with each passing day.

11. Balancing Independence and Togetherness

As Ryan and Emily settled into their life together, they learned the importance of balancing their independence with their togetherness. They both had busy careers and interests outside of their relationship, and they knew that it was important to maintain their own sense of identity and autonomy.

At the same time, they cherished their time together and made sure to prioritize their relationship. They found ways to enjoy each other's company while still pursuing their individual goals and passions.

For example, Ryan loved to go on long runs and hikes, while Emily enjoyed practicing yoga and taking dance classes. They made sure to carve out time for these activities on their own, while also finding ways to incorporate them into their time together.

Sometimes they would go for a run or hike together, pushing each other to go further and faster. Other times, Emily would teach Ryan some yoga poses, or they would take a dance class together.

They also found ways to support each other's career ambitions. Ryan was a successful entrepreneur, while Emily was a talented artist. They both understood the demands of their respective fields and made sure to give each other space and support when needed.

At the same time, they enjoyed collaborating on creative projects together, such as designing the layout of Ryan's new office space or creating a mural for a local art festival.

Through it all, they remained committed to each other and to their relationship, knowing that their love was strong enough to withstand any challenge or obstacle that came their way. They knew that their balance of independence and togetherness was what made their relationship thrive, and they worked hard to maintain that balance every day.

One evening, as they were sitting on the couch after a long day, Ryan turned to Emily and said, "You know, I'm so grateful for how we balance each other out. I feel like we can pursue our own interests and passions while still being there for each other."

Emily smiled and nodded, "I feel the same way. I love that we can support each other in our careers and hobbies while also making time for each other."

Ryan took her hand and said, "I think that's what makes our relationship so strong. We're not dependent on each other for everything, but we still value and prioritize our time together."

Emily leaned in and kissed him, "I couldn't agree more. I think we have something really special here."

They cuddled up on the couch, feeling content and grateful for the balance they had found in their relationship. They knew that there would always be ups and downs, but they were confident that they could weather any storm as long as they had each other.

As they sat there, enjoying each other's company, Ryan suddenly turned to Emily with a mischievous look on his face.

"You know what we should do?" he asked.

"What?" Emily replied, curious.

"We should plan a big trip together. Something adventurous and exciting, like hiking in the Andes or exploring the Amazon rainforest."

Emily's eyes widened with excitement. "That sounds amazing! When would we go?"

Ryan grinned. "How about next summer? We can start planning and saving now."

Emily hugged him, feeling grateful for his spontaneous and adventurous spirit. "I love that idea. Let's do it."

And so, they began planning their big adventure together, researching destinations, booking flights and accommodations, and preparing for the journey of a lifetime. As they worked together, they felt their connection deepening even further, knowing that they were embarking on this new adventure as a team.

12. Managing Differences

As Ryan and Emily's relationship continued to grow, they began to encounter new challenges. Despite their strong connection, they couldn't deny that they had different perspectives and ways of approaching certain situations. It wasn't always easy to manage their differences, but they were committed to finding a way to work through them.

One day, they had a heated argument over a decision they needed to make about their finances. Ryan was more risk-averse and wanted to save more money for the future, while Emily was more willing to take risks and wanted to invest more in their present experiences.

As they talked, their voices grew louder and more frustrated. Finally, Ryan threw up his hands and said, "I just don't understand why you're so willing to take risks. Can't you see that we need to be responsible and plan for our future?"

Emily felt her own frustration rising, but she took a deep breath and tried to stay calm. "I understand your perspective, but I also think that we need to live our lives and not just save for the future. I don't want to look back in 20 years and regret not taking more chances."

They both fell silent, feeling stuck and unsure of how to move forward. But then, Ryan spoke up again, this time with a softer tone. "I hear what you're saying, and I do want to enjoy our lives together. Maybe we can find a way to balance our priorities and make sure that we're both happy and fulfilled."

Emily nodded, feeling relieved that Ryan was willing to consider her perspective as well. They continued to talk and work through their differences, coming up with a plan that satisfied both of them.

Through this experience, Ryan and Emily learned that managing differences in a relationship wasn't about avoiding conflict altogether, but rather about finding a way to communicate and compromise. They knew that they would continue to encounter challenges, but they were confident in their ability to work through them as a team.

As they navigated more disagreements and differences, Ryan and Emily found that communication was key to resolving their conflicts.

One evening, they were discussing their plans for the weekend. Emily wanted to go on a hike with some friends, but Ryan had been looking forward to a relaxing weekend at home. As they talked, Ryan started to feel frustrated and resentful, feeling like Emily was always making plans without considering his preferences.

"I don't understand why you can't just stay home with me," Ryan said, his voice tinged with annoyance.

Emily could sense Ryan's frustration, but she also felt hurt and misunderstood. "I want to spend time with my friends, and I don't think that means I'm not prioritizing our relationship," she said.

Ryan sighed. "I know, but sometimes it feels like you're always making plans without considering how I feel. I want to be a part of your life, but it's hard when you're always doing your own thing."

Emily nodded thoughtfully, understanding where Ryan was coming from. "I hear you, and I do want to make sure that we're both happy and connected. Maybe we can find a way to balance our individual needs with our relationship needs."

They continued to talk and brainstorm ways to balance their individual desires with their commitment to their relationship. They eventually came up with a compromise where Emily would go on the hike but they would plan a special date night the following weekend.

Through this conversation, Ryan and Emily learned that their individual needs and desires were important, but so was their commitment to each other. They realized that they needed to communicate their needs and concerns in a way that was respectful and empathetic, and that finding a compromise was always possible.

As their relationship continued to grow and deepen, Ryan and Emily found that their ability to manage their differences strengthened their bond even more. They knew that their relationship wasn't perfect, but they were committed to working through any challenges that came their way.

Over time, Ryan and Emily developed a deep sense of trust and understanding in their relationship. They knew that they could count on each other to be there through both the good times and the bad.

One day, Ryan came to Emily with some difficult news. His mother had been diagnosed with a serious illness and he was struggling to cope with the news. Emily listened patiently as Ryan opened up about his fears and worries.

"I don't know what to do," Ryan said, his voice shaking. "I feel like I'm falling apart."

Emily took his hand and squeezed it gently. "I'm here for you, no matter what," she said. "We'll get through this together."

Over the next few weeks, Emily was there for Ryan every step of the way as he supported his mother through her illness. She listened as he talked about his fears and worries, and she provided comfort and support when he needed it most.

Through this experience, Ryan and Emily learned the power of vulnerability and the importance of being there for each other during difficult times. They realized that their love for each other was stronger than any challenge they might face, and that they could overcome anything as long as they had each other.

As they celebrated their two-year anniversary, Ryan and Emily looked back on all that they had been through together. They knew that their relationship wasn't perfect, but they were proud of how far they had come and excited for all the adventures that lay ahead.

"We've been through so much together," Ryan said, his eyes filled with love and admiration for Emily. "I can't imagine my life without you."

Emily smiled, feeling the same way. "I love you so much," she said. "Here's to many more years together."

Ryan and Emily spent the rest of the night reminiscing about their favorite moments from the past two years. They talked about the time they went camping in the mountains and got caught in a thunderstorm, and the time they took a road trip down the coast and stumbled upon a hidden beach.

As they talked, Ryan and Emily realized that they had built a life together filled with adventure, love, and mutual respect. They had learned to balance their independence and togetherness, and had grown even closer through the challenges they had faced.

The next day, Ryan surprised Emily with a trip to a hot air balloon festival that they had talked about attending for years. As they soared above the clouds, looking down at the colorful balloons below, Ryan turned to Emily and said, "I'm so grateful for you and all the joy you bring to my life."

Emily leaned in for a kiss, feeling overwhelmed with love and gratitude for the man sitting next to her. As they touched down on the ground, hand in hand, Ryan and Emily knew that they were ready for whatever came next in their journey together.

Over the years, Ryan and Emily continued to face challenges and obstacles, but they always found a way to come out stronger on the other side. They learned that love wasn't always easy, but it was always worth fighting for.

As they looked back on their lives together, they were proud of all they had accomplished and all they had overcome. And as they looked ahead, hand in hand, they knew that their love would continue to grow and thrive for years to come.

13. Navigating Family Dynamics

Ryan and Emily had always been close with their families, but they quickly realized that merging their families was a whole new challenge. Ryan's family was very traditional and conservative, while Emily's family was more liberal and laid-back. As they began planning their wedding, tensions began to rise between the families.

Ryan and Emily knew that they needed to find a way to navigate the family dynamics if they were going to have a successful wedding and marriage. They started by having an open and honest conversation with each other about their expectations and concerns.

"I know that my family can be difficult sometimes," Ryan said, "but I want to make sure that they feel included and respected."

Emily nodded. "I understand, but I also want to make sure that my family feels comfortable and not judged for being different."

Ryan and Emily decided to sit down with both families together and have a frank discussion about their hopes for the wedding and their expectations for how everyone would behave. It was a difficult conversation, but they both felt relieved to have everything out in the open.

As the wedding approached, Ryan and Emily's families slowly began to come together. They realized that they had more in common than they initially thought and that their differences could be celebrated rather than feared.

At the wedding, Ryan's conservative uncle surprised everyone by giving a heartfelt toast about the importance of love and acceptance, while Emily's liberal aunt led the whole reception in a dance to a popular pop song.

Ryan and Emily knew that navigating family dynamics was an ongoing process, but they were grateful to have started their marriage with a strong foundation of communication, understanding, and acceptance.

After the wedding, Ryan and Emily continued to make an effort to balance their families' expectations and traditions. They made sure to spend time with both families during holidays and special occasions, and they always made an effort to include everyone in their plans.

As they started their own family, Ryan and Emily also had to navigate the new dynamics of being parents. They had different parenting styles and ideas about how to raise their children, but they worked together to find a common ground.

Ryan wanted their children to have structure and discipline, while Emily wanted to encourage their creativity and independence. They realized that they needed to find a way to balance both approaches and create a parenting style that worked for both of them and their children.

They took parenting classes together and read books on child development, and they also sought advice from their own parents and other parents they trusted. They learned to compromise and communicate effectively, and they were able to raise their children in a loving and supportive environment.

As their children grew older and started their own families, Ryan and Emily continued to prioritize their relationships with their families. They made sure to be involved in their children's lives and support them in any way they could, while also respecting their independence and autonomy.

Ryan and Emily knew that family dynamics would always be a part of their lives, but they were confident in their ability to navigate them with grace and understanding. They had learned that building strong relationships with their families required patience, compromise, and most importantly, love.

Ryan and Emily were sitting at the kitchen table, looking through old family photo albums. They were reminiscing about their childhoods and the memories they had with their families.

"I can't believe how much time has passed," Emily said with a sigh.

"I know, it feels like just yesterday we were kids running around in our parents' backyards," Ryan replied.

Emily smiled. "Those were good times."

Ryan nodded in agreement. "Yeah, they were. And it's important to us that we continue to create good memories with our own families."

Emily put down the photo album and looked at Ryan. "I agree, but it's not always easy. Our families have different expectations and traditions, and it can be hard to balance everything."

Ryan took her hand. "I know, but we've come this far by communicating and compromising. We can continue to do that, and we'll figure it out together."

Emily smiled. "You're right. We've always been a good team."

They both knew that navigating family dynamics would continue to be a challenge, but they were committed to working together to create a happy and loving family. They knew that building strong relationships with their families required time, effort, and understanding, but they were willing to do whatever it took to make it work.

14. Overcoming Insecurities

As their relationship continued to deepen, Ryan and Emily found themselves confronting insecurities that they had never before acknowledged. They had always been honest with each other, but they were beginning to realize that there were parts of themselves that they had been afraid to share.

One day, as they were sitting on the couch together, Ryan turned to Emily and said, "There's something I need to tell you."

Emily looked at him, concerned. "What is it?"

"I've been struggling with insecurities lately," Ryan said. "I worry that I'm not good enough for you, or that you'll realize one day that you can do better."

Emily's heart sank. "Ryan, I love you. You are more than enough for me."

"I know, but it's hard to shake those feelings," Ryan said.

Emily took his hand. "I understand. I've been struggling with my own insecurities, too. Sometimes I worry that I'm not doing enough to make you happy, or that you'll get bored of me."

Ryan looked at her with surprise. "Really? I could never get bored of you, Emily. You make me so happy."

"I know, but sometimes my mind just goes to those places," Emily said with a sigh.

Ryan pulled her closer to him. "We're in this together, Em. We can help each other overcome these insecurities and remind each other how much we love and appreciate each other."

Emily smiled and leaned into him. "You're right. We're a team."

From that moment on, Ryan and Emily made a conscious effort to communicate openly and honestly about their insecurities. They reminded each other of their love and support, and they worked together to overcome their fears and doubts. It wasn't always easy, but they knew that they could face anything as long as they were together.

Over time, Ryan and Emily began to develop a deeper sense of trust and security in their relationship. They were no longer afraid to share their vulnerabilities with each other, and they knew that they could count on each other for support and understanding.

As they worked through their insecurities, they also began to recognize the ways in which their past experiences and relationships had influenced their fears and doubts. Ryan had struggled with feelings of inadequacy since childhood, while Emily had been hurt by past relationships that had left her feeling unworthy of love.

Together, they learned to recognize and challenge these negative thought patterns, and to build each other up with positive affirmations and reassurances.

Through their commitment to overcoming their insecurities, Ryan and Emily found a deeper level of intimacy and connection than they had ever thought possible. They knew that they were stronger together than they could ever be apart.

As they looked to the future, they knew that there would be challenges and obstacles ahead, but they felt confident that they could face them together with the love and support they had built between them.

With a deep sense of gratitude and appreciation for each other, Ryan and Emily celebrated the milestones they had achieved in their journey, and looked forward to the ones that were yet to come.

Ryan and Emily sat on the couch, their hands intertwined as they talked about their insecurities.

Ryan sighed heavily. "I know it's silly, but sometimes I feel like I'm not good enough for you. Like you deserve someone better."

Emily squeezed his hand. "You're more than good enough for me, Ryan. You're amazing. You make me laugh, you're supportive, and you're always there for me when I need you. I couldn't ask for anything more."

"But what if I mess up? What if I let you down?" Ryan's voice was filled with doubt.

Emily leaned in closer. "We all make mistakes, Ryan. But I trust you, and I know that you always try your best. And even if you do mess up, I'll still love you."

Ryan smiled at her, feeling a sense of relief wash over him. "Thank you, Emily. You always know how to make me feel better."

Emily chuckled. "That's what partners are for, right?"

They sat in silence for a few moments, enjoying each other's company.

Finally, Ryan spoke up again. "What about you, Emily? What are your insecurities?"

Emily hesitated for a moment before answering. "I've had some bad relationships in the past, and sometimes I worry that I'm not worthy of love. That maybe I'm not enough."

Ryan's heart ached for her. "Emily, you are more than enough. You are beautiful, intelligent, and kind. And most importantly, you are worthy of love. I love you for who you are, flaws and all."

Tears pricked at Emily's eyes as she looked at him. "Thank you, Ryan. I needed to hear that."

They held each other tightly, their love and support for each other strengthening with each passing moment.

Ryan and Emily sat on the couch, their hands intertwined as they talked about their insecurities.

Ryan sighed heavily. "I know it's silly, but sometimes I feel like I'm not good enough for you. Like you deserve someone better."

Emily squeezed his hand. "You're more than good enough for me, Ryan. You're amazing. You make me laugh, you're supportive, and you're always there for me when I need you. I couldn't ask for anything more."

"But what if I mess up? What if I let you down?" Ryan's voice was filled with doubt.

Emily leaned in closer. "We all make mistakes, Ryan. But I trust you, and I know that you always try your best. And even if you do mess up, I'll still love you."

Ryan smiled at her, feeling a sense of relief wash over him. "Thank you, Emily. You always know how to make me feel better."

Emily chuckled. "That's what partners are for, right?"

They sat in silence for a few moments, enjoying each other's company.

Finally, Ryan spoke up again. "What about you, Emily? What are your insecurities?"

Emily hesitated for a moment before answering. "I've had some bad relationships in the past, and sometimes I worry that I'm not worthy of love. That maybe I'm not enough."

Ryan's heart ached for her. "Emily, you are more than enough. You are beautiful, intelligent, and kind. And most importantly, you are worthy of love. I love you for who you are, flaws and all."

Tears pricked at Emily's eyes as she looked at him. "Thank you, Ryan. I needed to hear that."

They held each other tightly, their love and support for each other strengthening with each passing moment.

When we last left off with Emily and Ryan, they were in the midst of a disagreement about their future plans. Emily had just expressed her desire to move to a new city for a job opportunity, but Ryan was hesitant about uprooting their lives.

Ryan sighed and ran a hand through his hair. "I just don't know, Em. It's not that I don't support you or your career aspirations, but it's a big decision to make. And what about our families? They all live here. What would we do without them?"

Emily took a deep breath and held Ryan's hand. "I understand your concerns, Ryan. And I appreciate your love for our families, but we can't let that hold us back from pursuing our dreams. I've always been upfront about my ambition and I don't want to compromise that."

Ryan nodded, "I know that, Em. And I don't want you to compromise your dreams either. But it's not just about us. We need to consider how this decision will impact our families too."

Emily paused for a moment, taking in Ryan's words. "You're right, Ryan. I didn't think about that. Maybe we can talk to our families and see if they can visit us often or if we can plan trips back home. We can make it work."

Ryan smiled, "That's a good idea, Em. I'm willing to talk to our families about this and see how we can make it work. But we need to make sure that we're doing what's best for both of us."

Emily hugged Ryan, feeling relieved that they were able to have an open and honest conversation about their future plans. She knew that it wouldn't be easy, but she was willing to work with Ryan to find a solution that worked for both of them.

Over the next few weeks, Emily and Ryan talked to their families about their plans to move to a new city. They were met with mixed reactions, but ultimately, their families supported their decision.

With their families' blessing, Emily and Ryan started to plan for their move. They researched the new city, looked for apartments, and talked about how they would manage their finances.

As they worked through the logistics, Emily and Ryan's relationship grew stronger. They learned to communicate effectively, compromise, and support each other's goals.

Finally, the day of their move arrived. Emily and Ryan stood in their empty apartment, surrounded by boxes and suitcases. They looked at each other, feeling excited and nervous for the adventure ahead.

Ryan took Emily's hand and said, "Are you ready?"

Emily smiled, "I'm ready, Ryan. Let's do this."

They walked out of their apartment, ready to start a new chapter in their lives together.

15. Making Sacrifices for Love

Emily and Ryan had been together for almost two years now, and things were going well for them. They had grown incredibly close, sharing intimate moments and creating wonderful memories together.

One day, Ryan came home from work looking troubled. Emily could tell that something was bothering him. She asked him what was wrong, and Ryan hesitated for a moment before finally admitting that he had been offered a job opportunity in another state.

Emily's heart sank. She loved Ryan so much, but the thought of him leaving her behind was unbearable. They had talked about the possibility of Ryan moving for work before, but they never thought it would actually happen.

Ryan could see the worry on Emily's face and tried to reassure her. "I know this is hard for us, but it's a great opportunity for my career. And who knows, maybe it could be a new adventure for us both."

Emily nodded, trying to hold back her tears. She knew that Ryan's job was important, but the thought of being apart from him was too much to bear. Ryan could see how upset she was and pulled her into a tight embrace.

"I promise we'll make it work. We can figure out a plan that works for both of us," he whispered into her ear.

Over the next few weeks, they talked about what it would mean for their relationship if Ryan moved. They decided that they didn't want to break up just because of distance, but they also knew that long-distance relationships could be challenging.

Ryan had to move in a month, so they didn't have much time to figure out their plan. Emily knew that she wanted to support Ryan and his career, but she also didn't want to give up her own life and career in their current city.

After many discussions and late-night phone calls, they came up with a compromise. Emily would stay in their current city and continue with her job, while Ryan would move to the other state and work on his new job. They agreed to visit each other as often as possible and to make the most of their time together.

The day of Ryan's move arrived, and Emily helped him pack up his things. They hugged each other tightly, both holding back tears. Ryan promised Emily that he would be back soon, and that they would make it work.

Over the next few months, Emily and Ryan talked almost every day, sharing stories about their new experiences and supporting each other through the challenges of long-distance.

Emily missed Ryan terribly, but she was also proud of him for pursuing his dreams. She threw herself into her work, trying to stay busy and distract herself from the loneliness she felt.

As the months went by, Emily and Ryan's visits became more frequent. They cherished every moment they had together, making sure to make the most of their time.

One day, Ryan surprised Emily by showing up at her doorstep unannounced. Emily was overjoyed to see him and pulled him into a tight embrace.

"I missed you so much," she said, tears streaming down her face.

"I missed you too," Ryan said, smiling. "I have something to show you."

He took Emily's hand and led her to the car. They drove to a nearby park, and Ryan pulled out a blanket and a picnic basket.

"This is just a little something I put together," he said, smiling. "I wanted to celebrate us and all that we've been through."

Emily felt a warmth in her heart, knowing how much effort Ryan had put into this surprise. They spent the afternoon in the park, enjoying each other's company and reminiscing about their time together.

As the sun started to set, Ryan pulled out a small box from his pocket. Emily's heart raced as she realized what was happening.

"Emily, you are the love of my life.

Emily was struggling to balance her demanding job with her relationship with Ryan. She had been working long hours at the office for several weeks now, and it was starting to take a toll on her. Ryan, on the other hand, had been working from home and had more flexibility in his schedule. He noticed that Emily was stressed out and exhausted, and he wanted to do something to help her.

One evening, as Emily was finishing up some work on her laptop, Ryan came up behind her and gently rubbed her shoulders. "You've been working so hard lately," he said softly. "Why don't you take a break and come watch a movie with me?"

Emily sighed and leaned back into Ryan's touch. "I wish I could, but I have so much work to do. I don't know how I'm going to get everything done."

Ryan sat down next to her and took her hand. "I understand that work is important to you, but so is our relationship. I don't want you to burn yourself out. How about we make a deal? You take the rest of the night off, and I'll help you catch up on your work tomorrow."

Emily looked at Ryan skeptically. "Are you serious? You would help me with my work?"

Ryan nodded. "Of course. I want to support you in any way I can. And besides, I'm pretty good with spreadsheets."

Emily couldn't help but smile at Ryan's offer. "Okay, you're on. But only if you promise not to get distracted by your video games."

Ryan laughed. "Deal."

The rest of the evening was spent snuggled up on the couch, watching a romantic comedy. Emily felt a sense of relief wash over her as she allowed herself to relax and enjoy the moment. She was grateful for Ryan's willingness to help her out and to make sacrifices for their relationship.

The next day, Ryan followed through on his promise and spent the day helping Emily catch up on her work. They worked side by side at the kitchen table, taking occasional breaks to chat and make each other laugh. By the end of the day, Emily was caught up on her work, and she felt a renewed sense of energy and motivation.

"Thank you so much for helping me out today," Emily said, giving Ryan a grateful hug.

Ryan hugged her back. "Anything for you, babe. I just want to see you happy and fulfilled, both in your work and in our relationship."

Emily smiled and kissed him on the cheek. "I am. Thanks to you."

Emily looked at Ryan with a mixture of surprise and admiration. "You would do that for me?" she asked, her voice shaking slightly.

Ryan took her hand in his and looked into her eyes. "Of course, Emily. I love you, and I want to do everything I can to make you happy."

Emily felt her heart swell with love for Ryan. She couldn't believe how lucky she was to have someone so caring and selfless in her life. "Thank you, Ryan," she said, leaning in to give him a kiss on the cheek. "I don't know what I would do without you."

Ryan smiled, feeling a warm sense of contentment in his chest. "You don't have to worry about that, Emily. I'll always be here for you."

As they sat together on the couch, Emily felt a wave of gratitude wash over her. She knew that Ryan was the one for her, and she was willing to make sacrifices for him too. It was a comforting thought to know that they were both in it for the long haul, no matter what obstacles they may face.

Over the next few months, Emily and Ryan continued to grow closer. They learned more about each other's likes and dislikes, and found ways to compromise when they didn't see eye-to-eye. They made an effort to spend time with each other's friends and family, and discovered that they had a lot in common when it came to values and beliefs.

But despite their strong bond, there were still moments of doubt and insecurity. Emily couldn't help but worry that something would come along and threaten their relationship, and Ryan struggled with feelings of inadequacy and fear of not being enough for Emily.

It was during one of these moments of doubt that Ryan decided to take action. He had been researching couples therapy online, and had come across a therapist who specialized in helping couples overcome insecurities and build stronger relationships.

He hesitated for a moment, wondering if Emily would be open to the idea. But ultimately, he decided that it was worth a try if it meant strengthening their bond.

"Emily," he said one evening as they were cooking dinner together. "There's something I want to talk to you about."

Emily turned to him, sensing the seriousness in his tone. "What is it?" she asked.

Ryan took a deep breath. "I've been thinking a lot lately about how much I care about you, and how much I want our relationship to last. But I know that we both have our insecurities, and I want us to work on them together."

Emily looked at him with a mix of surprise and curiosity. "What do you mean?"

Ryan took out his phone and pulled up the website for the couples therapist he had found. "I came across this therapist who specializes in helping couples overcome insecurities and build stronger relationships. I was thinking that maybe we could give it a try."

Emily felt a twinge of nervousness in her stomach. The idea of opening up about her insecurities to a stranger was daunting, but she knew that Ryan was right. They needed to address these issues if they wanted their relationship to thrive.

After some discussion, they decided to book an appointment with the therapist. The first session was nerve-wracking, but they both felt relieved to have a safe space to talk about their feelings and work on strategies for overcoming their insecurities.

Over the next few weeks, they attended weekly sessions and worked through a variety of issues. They learned how to communicate more effectively, how to give each other space when needed, and how to express their needs and wants in a healthy way.

It wasn't easy, and there were times when they felt frustrated or discouraged. But as they continued to put in the work, they began to see tangible results. They

16. Learning to Apologize

Emily sat on the couch, staring blankly at the TV screen as Ryan paced back and forth in front of her.

"I can't believe I said that to you," Ryan said, running his hands through his hair. "I'm so sorry, Emily. I don't know what came over me."

Emily didn't respond, still feeling hurt and angry from Ryan's hurtful words. She had never seen this side of him before and wasn't sure how to react.

"I know I messed up," Ryan continued, still pacing. "But please, can we talk about it? I want to make things right between us."

Emily took a deep breath and finally spoke. "I appreciate your apology, Ryan. But I need some time to process this. I don't know if I can just forgive and forget so easily."

Ryan nodded understandingly. "I understand. Take all the time you need. I'll do anything to make it up to you."

The next few days were tense between Emily and Ryan. They barely spoke to each other, and when they did, it was brief and awkward. Emily couldn't shake the hurtful things Ryan had said, and Ryan felt guilty and ashamed for his behavior.

One night, as they were sitting down to dinner, Ryan finally broke the silence. "Emily, I know I messed up big time, and I can't keep apologizing forever. What can I do to make it up to you?"

Emily took a deep breath, unsure of what to say. "I don't know, Ryan. It's not just about the words you said. It's about the way you made me feel. How can I trust that you won't do something like that again?"

Ryan nodded thoughtfully. "I understand. Maybe we can start by setting some ground rules for how we communicate with each other. I don't want to ever make you feel like that again, Emily."

Emily looked at him, surprised by his sincerity. "Okay," she said finally. "Let's start there."

Over the next few weeks, Emily and Ryan worked on their communication skills. They learned to listen to each other without interrupting, and to express their feelings without resorting to hurtful words. It wasn't easy, but they both knew that it was necessary if they wanted to have a healthy, long-lasting relationship.

Slowly but surely, Emily began to trust Ryan again. She saw the effort he was making and appreciated his willingness to change. And Ryan was grateful for the chance to prove himself to Emily and to become a better partner.

In the end, their relationship grew stronger because of their willingness to acknowledge their mistakes and work towards a better future together.

Emily took a deep breath and looked at Ryan. "I'm sorry," she said, "I shouldn't have said that. I know you're doing your best."

Ryan sighed and looked at her. "It's okay," he said, "I know it's frustrating for you too."

Emily nodded. "I just hate seeing you so stressed out all the time. I wish there was something I could do to help."

Ryan smiled at her. "Just being here with me helps," he said, "I don't know what I'd do without you."

Emily smiled back at him. "I'll always be here for you," she said, "no matter what."

They sat in silence for a few moments, just enjoying each other's company. Then Ryan spoke up.

"You know," he said, "I've been thinking about something. I know we've talked about moving in together before, but maybe now's not the best time."

Emily looked at him, surprised. "Really?" she said, "I thought you were excited about the idea."

"I am," Ryan said quickly, "but with everything that's been going on, I don't want to add more stress to our lives. And we're both still getting our careers off the ground. It might be better to wait a little longer."

Emily nodded thoughtfully. "I see what you mean," she said, "but it's not like we're rushing into anything. We've been together for almost two years now."

"I know," Ryan said, "but I want to make sure we're both ready. Moving in together is a big step."

Emily took a deep breath and smiled at him. "You're right," she said, "I'm glad we're on the same page about this. And whenever we do decide to take that step, I know we'll be ready for it."

Ryan smiled back at her. "Me too," he said.

They hugged each other tightly, both feeling grateful for the love and understanding they shared.

As the months passed, Emily and Ryan continued to grow closer. They supported each other through the ups and downs of their careers, and made time for each other even when their schedules were packed. They learned to communicate more effectively and to be vulnerable with each other.

One evening, they were out for a walk in the park when Ryan stopped and took Emily's hand. "There's something I want to talk to you about," he said.

Emily looked at him, curious. "What is it?" she asked.

Ryan took a deep breath. "I've been thinking a lot about our future together," he said, "and I want you to know that I'm committed to making this work. I love you, Emily, and I want to spend the rest of my life with you."

Emily's eyes widened in surprise and delight. "Ryan," she said, her voice shaking, "are you saying what I think you're saying?"

Ryan nodded, a smile spreading across his face. "I'm saying that I want to marry you, Emily. Will you marry me?"

Tears welled up in Emily's eyes as she threw her arms around Ryan. "Yes," she said, "of course I will. I love you too."

They hugged each other tightly, both feeling overwhelmed with happiness and joy.

Over the next few months, they planned their wedding, which would take place in the same park where Ryan had proposed. They invited their closest friends and family members, and worked together to create a beautiful ceremony that reflected their love and commitment to each other.

As they stood together, holding hands and exchanging vows, Emily and Ryan knew that they were meant to be together. They had overcome obstacles, learned to communicate and trust each other, and grown into a deep.

Ryan let out a deep sigh, "I know. I should have apologized earlier, but I was so caught up in my own emotions that I didn't realize how much I was hurting you. I'm sorry for being so selfish."

Emily looked at Ryan with a soft expression, "I appreciate you apologizing, and I forgive you. But you need to understand that communication is key in any relationship. We need to be able to talk about our feelings and be honest with each other."

Ryan nodded, "You're right, and I promise to be more open with you. I don't want to lose you over something that could have been easily resolved with a conversation."

Emily smiled, "I don't want to lose you either, Ryan. We both need to put effort into our relationship and work through any challenges that come our way. Together."

They shared a hug, feeling a renewed sense of closeness and understanding between them. From that moment on, they made an effort to communicate more openly and honestly with each other, and their relationship flourished.

As time went on, Ryan and Emily faced many more challenges and obstacles in their relationship, but they always worked through them together, with honesty, understanding, and love. They knew that their love for each other was worth fighting for, and they never gave up on each other.

Years later, on a warm summer evening, Ryan got down on one knee and proposed to Emily, surrounded by their closest friends and family. With tears in her eyes, Emily said yes, and they began a new chapter of their lives together, filled with love, trust, and endless adventure.

Looking back on their journey together, Ryan and Emily realized that their love story wasn't just about falling in love, but about growing together, learning from each other, and never giving up on each other, no matter what challenges they faced. They knew that their love would continue to grow stronger with each passing day, and they were excited to see where life would take them next, together.

17. Forgiveness and Healing

Emily sat on the couch, tears streaming down her face as Ryan tried to comfort her. "I can't believe I did this to us," she said between sobs. "I'm so sorry."

Ryan rubbed her back gently. "It's okay, Em. We'll get through this."

"I don't know how you can even look at me right now," Emily said, wiping her tears away. "I feel so ashamed."

Ryan took her hand. "You made a mistake, but that doesn't mean I love you any less. We'll work through it together."

Emily sniffled. "I just don't know how to move past this. How can you forgive me?"

Ryan sighed. "Forgiveness isn't about forgetting what happened or pretending like it didn't hurt. It's about acknowledging what happened, taking responsibility, and choosing to move forward despite the pain."

"But how can I even begin to make it up to you?" Emily asked.

Ryan smiled softly. "You don't have to make it up to me. I forgive you because I love you, not because of anything you can do to make it right."

Emily leaned her head on his shoulder. "I love you too, Ryan."

They sat in silence for a few minutes before Ryan spoke up. "Do you want to talk about what happened?"

Emily nodded. "I just feel so stupid. I was out with some friends, and we got drunk. I don't even remember all of it, but I know I ended up kissing one of them."

Ryan's expression darkened. "Who was it?"

Emily hesitated. "It doesn't matter. He's just a friend."

"It does matter, Emily," Ryan said firmly. "I need to know who it was."

Emily sighed. "It was Mark."

Ryan's eyes widened in shock. "Mark? The guy you've been friends with since college?"

Emily nodded. "I know, I know. It's so stupid. I don't even know why I did it."

Ryan took a deep breath. "Okay. We'll deal with that later. Right now, we need to focus on healing and moving forward."

Emily looked up at him with tear-filled eyes. "Thank you, Ryan. I don't deserve your forgiveness."

Ryan squeezed her hand. "That's the thing about love, Em. It's not about deserving. It's about giving and receiving."

Emily leaned in for a hug, and Ryan held her tightly. As they sat there, wrapped up in each other's arms, they both knew that forgiveness and healing would take time, but they were willing to put in the work to save their relationship.

As time passed, Emily and Ryan continued to work on their relationship, rebuilding the trust and intimacy that they had once shared. They attended couples therapy regularly and had open and honest conversations about their feelings and concerns.

One day, during a therapy session, Emily spoke about the pain and hurt that she had been carrying with her since the betrayal. Ryan listened intently as she spoke, tears streaming down her face.

"I just don't know if I can ever fully trust you again," Emily said, her voice cracking with emotion.

"I understand that, and I'm sorry," Ryan replied. "But I want you to know that I love you more than anything in this world. I will do whatever it takes to make things right between us."

Emily took a deep breath and wiped away her tears. "I know you do, and I love you too," she said softly.

Over time, Ryan showed Emily that he was committed to making things right. He made sacrifices for her and their relationship, and was patient and understanding when Emily struggled with trust and forgiveness.

Slowly but surely, Emily began to feel that she could trust Ryan again. They started to make plans for the future, talking about buying a house together and starting a family.

One evening, as they sat on the couch together, Emily turned to Ryan and said, "I want you to know that I forgive you. It's not easy, and there will still be times when I feel hurt or angry, but I am willing to work through those feelings with you. I want to move forward and build a future together."

Ryan took her hand and squeezed it tightly. "Thank you," he said, his voice choked with emotion. "I will do everything in my power to make sure that you never regret giving me another chance."

From that moment on, Emily and Ryan worked tirelessly to build a strong, healthy, and loving relationship. They continued to attend therapy, communicate openly and honestly, and make sacrifices for each other.

Years later, as they stood together on their wedding day, Emily looked into Ryan's eyes and knew that he was the love of her life. She knew that they had been through difficult times, but that they had emerged stronger and more committed than ever before.

As they exchanged their vows, Emily knew that they had both learned the importance of forgiveness and healing, and that they would always work together to overcome any obstacle that came their way.

18. Overcoming a Rough Patch

Emily and Ryan had been together for over a year now, and things had been going well for them. They had learned to communicate effectively, had deepened their connection, and had celebrated many milestones together.

However, as with any relationship, they faced some challenges along the way. One of those challenges came in the form of a rough patch that they hit a few months into their relationship.

It all started when Emily began feeling overwhelmed with work and school. She was juggling a full-time job and a full course load, and she felt like she was barely keeping her head above water. She started canceling plans with Ryan, and when they did spend time together, she was distracted and irritable.

Ryan tried to be understanding and supportive, but after a while, he started feeling neglected and unimportant. He didn't want to add to Emily's stress, but he also didn't want to be pushed aside. He started feeling resentful, and he didn't know how to talk to Emily about it without making things worse.

One night, after Emily had canceled plans with Ryan for the third time in a row, he finally confronted her about how he was feeling.

"Emily, I know you're really busy with work and school, but I feel like you're pulling away from me. I don't want to be a burden, but I miss spending time with you, and I feel like you're not making me a priority anymore," he said.

Emily looked guilty and ashamed. "I'm sorry, Ryan. I know I've been really distant lately. I'm just so stressed out with everything that's going on, and I feel like I'm drowning. I didn't mean to push you away."

Ryan nodded, understandingly. "I know, and I don't want to add to your stress. But I also don't want to be pushed aside. Can we figure out a way to balance everything and still make time for each other?"

Emily nodded, tears welling up in her eyes. "I want to make things work between us. I'll try to be more mindful of how I'm treating you and make more of an effort to prioritize our time together."

They hugged, and Ryan felt a weight lifted off his chest. He knew that it wouldn't be easy, but he was committed to working through this rough patch with Emily.

Over the next few weeks, they made a conscious effort to communicate more openly and honestly about their feelings and to make time for each other despite their busy schedules. It wasn't always perfect, but they were making progress.

One day, as they were snuggled up on the couch watching a movie, Emily turned to Ryan and said, "Thank you for being patient with me during that rough patch. I know I wasn't easy to be around, but I appreciate your support and understanding."

Ryan smiled and kissed her forehead. "Of course, Em. We're in this together, through the good times and the bad. And honestly, going through that rough patch made us stronger in the end."

Emily nodded in agreement, feeling grateful for the love and commitment they shared. They had overcome a challenge together, and they knew that they could overcome anything as long as they had each other.

Emily took a deep breath and looked at Ryan, "I think we need to talk."

Ryan nodded, his expression concerned. "What's going on?"

Emily hesitated for a moment, trying to find the right words. "I've been feeling like something's off between us lately."

Ryan frowned, "What do you mean?"

"It's just that we've been so busy with work and everything, and we haven't really had much time for each other," Emily explained. "And when we do spend time together, it feels like we're not really connecting like we used to."

Ryan sighed and nodded, "I know what you mean. I've been feeling the same way."

Emily looked at him, surprised. "Really?"

"Yeah," Ryan said, looking at her earnestly. "I've been so focused on work and other things that I haven't been putting in the effort to make our relationship a priority."

Emily felt a wave of relief wash over her. She had been worried that she was the only one feeling this way, but hearing Ryan's words made her feel like they were in this together.

"What do we do now?" she asked.

Ryan took her hand and gave it a reassuring squeeze. "We need to make more time for each other, and really make an effort to connect. Maybe we can plan a weekend away, just the two of us."

Emily smiled, feeling a sense of hope for the first time in a while. "I would love that."

Ryan leaned in and kissed her softly, and Emily felt a spark of the old magic between them.

Over the next few weeks, they made a concerted effort to spend more time together. They planned date nights, went on hikes, and even took a weekend trip to a nearby beach town.

It wasn't always easy – they both had demanding jobs and busy schedules – but they made a commitment to each other to prioritize their relationship.

As they reconnected and grew closer, Emily and Ryan found that they were able to weather the challenges and stresses of life with more grace and ease. They learned that making their relationship a priority was not just a nice idea, but a necessary ingredient for a happy and healthy life.

19. Making Plans for the Future

As Emily and Ryan continued to build their relationship, they began discussing their plans for the future. They talked about everything from career goals to family aspirations.

"I can't believe how lucky I am to have found you," Ryan said, holding Emily's hand as they walked along the beach.

Emily smiled. "I feel the same way. It's crazy to think about all the chances we had to never meet each other."

Ryan nodded. "But we did meet, and I'm so grateful for that. And now, I can't imagine my future without you in it."

Emily's heart swelled with happiness. "Me too. I love you so much."

"I love you too," Ryan replied.

As they continued their walk, they talked about their plans for the future. Emily shared her dream of opening her own bakery someday, and Ryan talked about his desire to travel more and see the world.

"I would love to see Europe someday," Ryan said.

Emily nodded. "Me too. And I would love to take you to Paris and try all the amazing pastries there."

Ryan smiled. "I'd be happy to be your taste tester."

They also talked about their family plans, and Ryan revealed that he wanted to have children someday.

"I want to have a big family," Ryan said. "I grew up with two brothers, and I loved it. I want our kids to have siblings to grow up with."

Emily smiled. "That sounds wonderful. I can't wait to start a family with you."

As they talked about their future plans, they realized how much they had in common and how well their goals aligned. They both wanted to travel, have successful careers, and start a family someday.

"I'm so excited for our future together," Emily said, leaning in to kiss Ryan.

"Me too," Ryan said, wrapping his arms around her.

As they sat on the beach, watching the sunset, they knew that they had a bright future ahead of them, filled with love, adventure, and endless possibilities.

Emily and Ryan spent a lot of time talking about their future plans. They discussed their career aspirations, where they wanted to live, and even started making plans for their wedding. Emily had always dreamed of a small, intimate ceremony with just their closest family and friends. Ryan had never given much thought to his wedding, but he was happy to go along with Emily's plans.

As they talked about their future, they realized that they had different ideas about where they wanted to live. Emily had always imagined living in a big city, while Ryan preferred a quieter, more rural setting. They discussed the pros and cons of each and tried to find a compromise that would make them both happy.

Eventually, they came up with a plan to live in a small town outside of a major city. This would give them the best of both worlds - the peace and quiet of a rural area, but still close enough to the city to take advantage of all it had to offer.

As they continued to plan for their future, they also talked about starting a family. Emily had always known she wanted to have children, and Ryan was excited at the idea of being a dad. They talked about how many children they wanted to have and what kind of parents they wanted to be.

They also discussed their career goals and how they could support each other in achieving them. Emily was determined to climb the corporate ladder and become a CEO someday, while Ryan wanted to start his own business. They talked about the challenges they would face and how they could help each other achieve their goals.

Finally, they talked about their dreams for retirement. Emily dreamed of traveling the world and experiencing different cultures, while Ryan wanted to live on a farm and raise animals. They joked about how they would spend their retirement years and promised to make each other's dreams come true.

As they finished their conversation, they both felt a sense of excitement and anticipation for what their future held. They knew that they had each other to rely on and support them through whatever challenges they may face.

Emily looked at Ryan and smiled. "I can't wait to spend the rest of my life with you," she said.

Ryan grinned back. "Me too," he replied. "I love you."

"I love you too," Emily said, as they embraced each other tightly.

Together, they knew that they could overcome any obstacle and build a life full of love and happiness.

Emily leaned in closer to Ryan, resting her head on his shoulder as they watched the sun set over the ocean.

Ryan put his arm around her, pulling her close. "I can't imagine my future without you," he said softly.

Emily smiled up at him. "I feel the same way. But what do you see for our future?"

Ryan thought for a moment. "I see us building a life together, maybe getting married one day. I see us traveling the world, experiencing new things together. And most importantly, I see us being happy and in love for the rest of our lives."

Emily's heart swelled with love for Ryan. "That sounds perfect," she said, snuggling even closer to him.

They sat in silence for a few moments, watching the sky turn from pink to orange to purple.

Finally, Emily broke the silence. "You know, I've been thinking about something lately."

"What's that?" Ryan asked.

"I've always wanted to start my own business," Emily said. "But I've been too afraid to take the risk."

Ryan looked at her with encouragement. "You should do it. I believe in you."

Emily smiled. "Thanks, Ryan. That means a lot to me."

Ryan looked out at the ocean, taking a deep breath. "There's something I've been meaning to tell you too."

"What is it?" Emily asked, turning to face him.

"I've been considering a job opportunity in a different city," Ryan said. "It would mean moving away from here."

Emily felt a pang of sadness in her chest. "Oh."

"But I want you to know that if I do take the job, I want you to come with me," Ryan said, taking her hand in his. "I can't imagine being apart from you."

Emily's heart swelled with love for Ryan. "I'll go with you, wherever you go," she said. "As long as we're together, that's all that matters to me."

Ryan smiled, pulling her close for a kiss as the sun disappeared below the horizon. They knew there would be challenges ahead, but they also knew that as long as they had each other, they could conquer anything.

Ryan smiled, his heart swelling with pride. "I can't wait to see you become a veterinarian, Em. I know you'll be amazing."

Emily blushed, feeling touched by Ryan's words. "Thanks, Ryan. And I can't wait to see you become a successful businessman."

Ryan chuckled. "I hope so. I've been working hard for it."

Emily's expression grew more serious. "Ryan, do you ever think about...us? Our future together?"

Ryan's heart rate quickened as he considered Emily's question. He knew that he loved her, but he also knew that they were still young and had a lot of growing to do. "I do, Em. But I also think we have a lot to figure out before we make any big decisions."

Emily nodded in agreement. "Yeah, you're right. I just want you to know that I love you and I see a future with you."

Ryan smiled, feeling a sense of comfort wash over him. "I love you too, Em. And I believe that we'll figure things out together."

As they continued to talk and make plans for their future, Ryan couldn't help but feel grateful for Emily's unwavering support and love. He knew that they had a long road ahead of them, but he was confident that they could face anything as long as they were together.

20. A Proposal and a Promise

It was a beautiful autumn day, with the sun shining brightly in the sky and a cool breeze blowing through the trees. Emily and Ryan were taking a walk in the park, enjoying the peacefulness of the day.

As they strolled along, Emily couldn't help but feel a sense of excitement and anticipation building inside of her. She knew that Ryan had something important to ask her, and she couldn't wait to find out what it was.

Finally, Ryan stopped walking and turned to face her. He took her hands in his and looked deeply into her eyes.

"Emily, I love you more than anything in this world," he began. "You are my best friend, my soulmate, and the love of my life. And I want to spend the rest of my life with you."

Emily's heart skipped a beat as she listened to Ryan's words. She felt tears prickling at the corners of her eyes, and her stomach was filled with butterflies.

"I want to ask you to be my wife," Ryan continued, dropping down on one knee and pulling out a small box from his pocket. "Will you marry me, Emily?"

Emily felt tears streaming down her face as she gazed at the beautiful ring that Ryan was holding out to her. It was simple yet elegant, and it sparkled in the sunlight.

"Yes, Ryan, I will marry you!" she exclaimed, throwing her arms around his neck and kissing him deeply.

As they embraced, Ryan whispered in her ear, "I promise to love you, cherish you, and support you through all the ups and downs of life. You are the most important thing to me, and I will always be by your side."

Emily smiled through her tears, feeling overwhelmed with love and happiness. She knew that life would not always be easy, but with Ryan by her side, she felt like she could conquer anything.

Together, they walked hand in hand out of the park, ready to start a new chapter in their lives.

Emily was overjoyed with Ryan's proposal, and she couldn't wait to spend the rest of her life with him. They spent the next few months planning their wedding, which they decided would take place in a beautiful garden.

As the day of the wedding drew closer, Emily and Ryan couldn't help but feel a bit nervous. They had been through so much together, and they wanted everything to be perfect on their special day.

The day of the wedding arrived, and Emily was a bundle of nerves as she got ready with her bridesmaids. When she finally walked down the aisle, she saw Ryan waiting for her at the altar, looking handsome and happy.

The ceremony was beautiful, and Emily and Ryan exchanged their vows in front of all of their loved ones. As they kissed for the first time as husband and wife, they knew that they had found true love.

After the ceremony, Emily and Ryan celebrated with their family and friends at the reception. They danced the night away and laughed until their sides hurt. As the night drew to a close, Emily and Ryan knew that they had made the right decision in choosing each other.

As they left the reception, hand in hand, Ryan whispered to Emily, "I promise to love you for the rest of my life, through thick and thin, for better or for worse."

Emily smiled and replied, "And I promise to do the same. I love you more than words can express."

As they drove away, Emily and Ryan knew that they had a lifetime of love and happiness ahead of them. They had overcome so many obstacles to get to this point, but they had done it together. They were ready for whatever the future held, as long as they were together.

Epilogue

As Emily stood at the altar, surrounded by her family and friends, she couldn't help but feel grateful for everything that had led her to this moment. She thought back on her journey with Ryan, and how they had overcome obstacles, learned to communicate and trust each other, and ultimately, fallen deeply in love.

She looked over at Ryan, who was beaming at her with pure happiness in his eyes. They had been through so much together, but it had all been worth it to get to this point.

As the ceremony began, Emily made a silent promise to herself and to Ryan. She promised to continue to work on their relationship, to communicate openly and honestly, to be vulnerable, and to never take their love for granted.

The rest of the day was a blur of happiness, laughter, and love. Emily and Ryan danced together, surrounded by their loved ones, and as they swayed to the music, Emily knew that this was just the beginning of their journey together.

In the years that followed, Emily and Ryan faced new challenges, but they faced them together. They traveled the world, bought a home, and started a family. They laughed, cried, and grew together, and their love only deepened with each passing day.

Looking back on their journey, Emily knew that meeting Ryan by chance had been the best thing that had ever happened to her. Their love story had been filled with ups and downs, but through it all, they had remained committed to each other.

As she lay in bed that night, surrounded by her family, Emily felt a sense of peace and contentment wash over her. She knew that no matter what the future held, she and Ryan would face it together, with love as their guiding force.

In conclusion, building and maintaining a healthy romantic relationship is not an easy task, but it can be one of the most rewarding experiences in life. It requires effort, commitment, communication, and understanding from both partners. The journey of Emily and Ryan showed how they faced various challenges and obstacles, but with determination and love, they were able to overcome them and grow stronger as a couple.

From their initial meeting by chance to their proposal and promise of a future together, Emily and Ryan's story highlights the importance of trust, vulnerability, compromise, and forgiveness in a relationship. They learned to communicate effectively, understand each other's needs, and support each other's dreams.

While every couple's journey may be different, the principles of a healthy relationship remain the same. It takes time, effort, and patience to build a strong foundation for a lasting and fulfilling romantic connection. And even after the proposal and the promise, the journey continues as couples face new challenges, milestones, and opportunities for growth.

Ultimately, a healthy and loving relationship is about two individuals coming together to share their lives and create a future filled with joy, love, and companionship.

Printed in Great Britain
by Amazon

22668654R10086